THE BEST OF
B.B. KING

ISBN 978-1-4234-9043-2

7777 W. BLUEMOUND RD. P.O. BOX 13819 MILWAUKEE, WI 53213

Visit Hal Leonard Online at
www.halleonard.com

AIN'T NOBODY HOME

Words and Music by
JERRY RAGAVOY

ASK ME NO QUESTIONS

Words and Music by
B.B. KING

You go out when you get read-y, and you come home _____ when you please. You just love me when you want to, ba-by, and you think it ought to be all right with me.

BE CAREFUL WITH A FOOL

Words and Music by B.B. KING
and JOE BIHARI

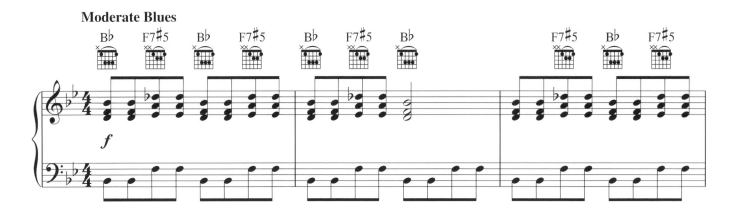

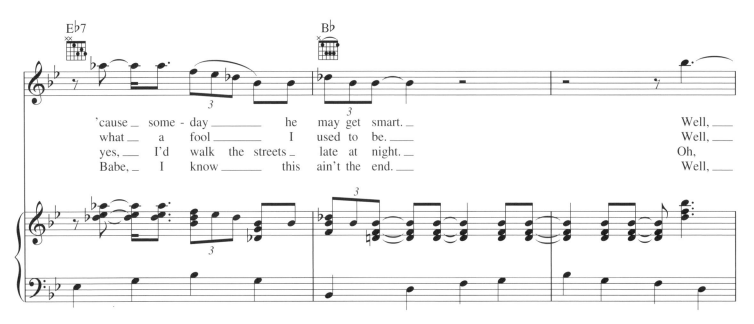

BEAUTICIAN BLUES

Words and Music by B.B. KING
and JULES BIHARI

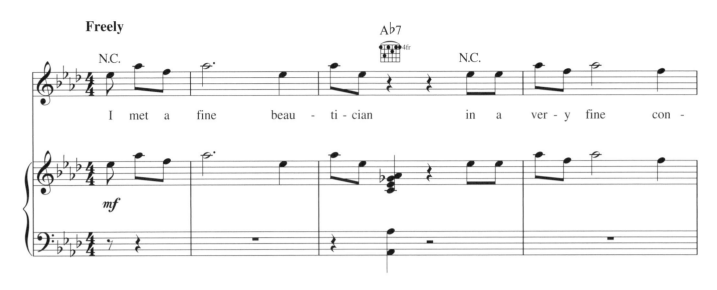

I met a fine beau-ti-cian in a ver-y fine con-

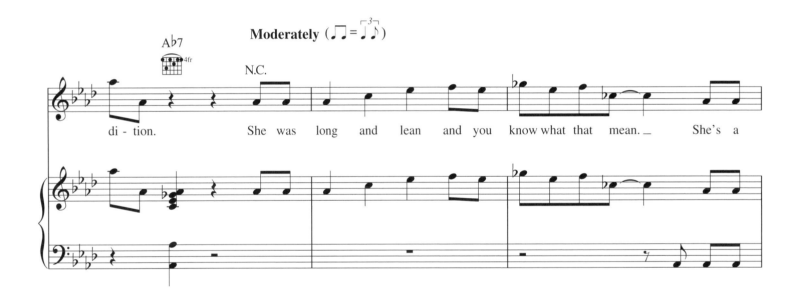

di-tion. She was long and lean and you know what that mean.__ She's a

good - lov-in' ma-ma, a hard - work-in' wom - an.

EVERYDAY I HAVE THE BLUES

Words and Music by
PETER CHATMAN

CHAINS AND THINGS

Words and Music by B.B. KING
and DAVE CLARK

Moderate Blues

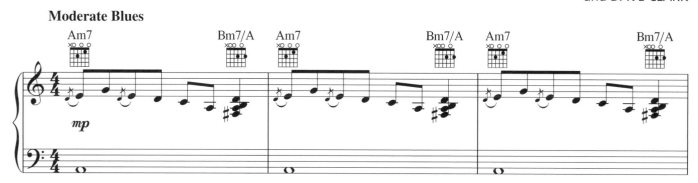

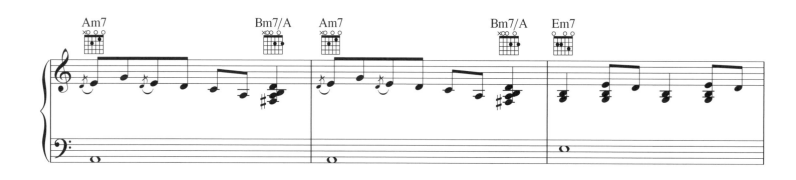

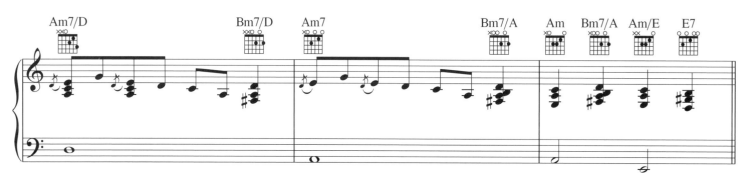

1. Woke up this morn - ing   af - ter 'noth - er one of those cra - zy dreams.
2. this morn - ing, __   seems like ev - 'ry - thing is _____ lost.
3. *Guitar solo*
4., 5. *(See additional lyrics)*

Oh, ____ noth - ing is
I've got a cold - heart -

go - ing right this __ morn - ing, __   the whole world _____ is wrong it
ed, wrong - do - ing __ wom - an, __   and a slave - driv - ing boss. _

seems.   Oh, I guess it's the
__   I can't __ lose these

Additional Lyrics

4. Well, you talk about hard luck and trouble,
   Seems to be my middle name.
   All the odds are against me,
   Yes, I can only play a losing game.
   These chains that bind me,
   Can't loosen these chains and things
   Just can't loosen these chains and things.

5. Oh, I would pack up and leave today, people,
   But I ain't got nowhere to go.
   Ain't got money to buy a ticket
   And I don't feel like walking anymore.
   These chains that bind me,
   I can't lose, I can't lose these chains and things.

CRYIN' WON'T HELP YOU

Words and Music by B.B. KING
and SAUL BIHARI

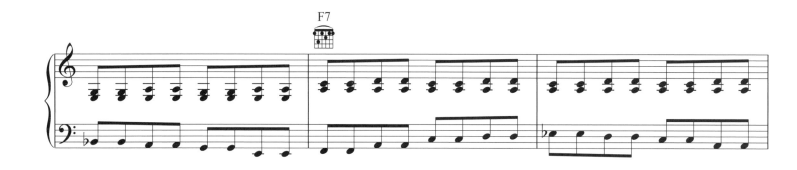

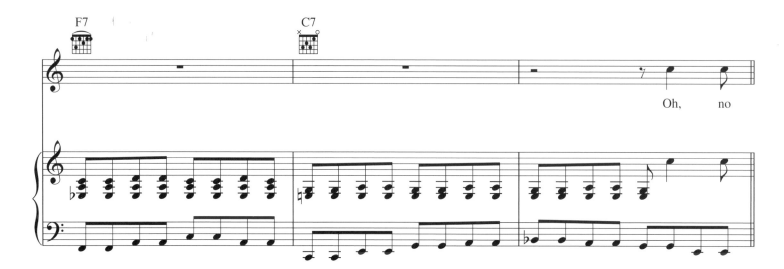

Oh, no

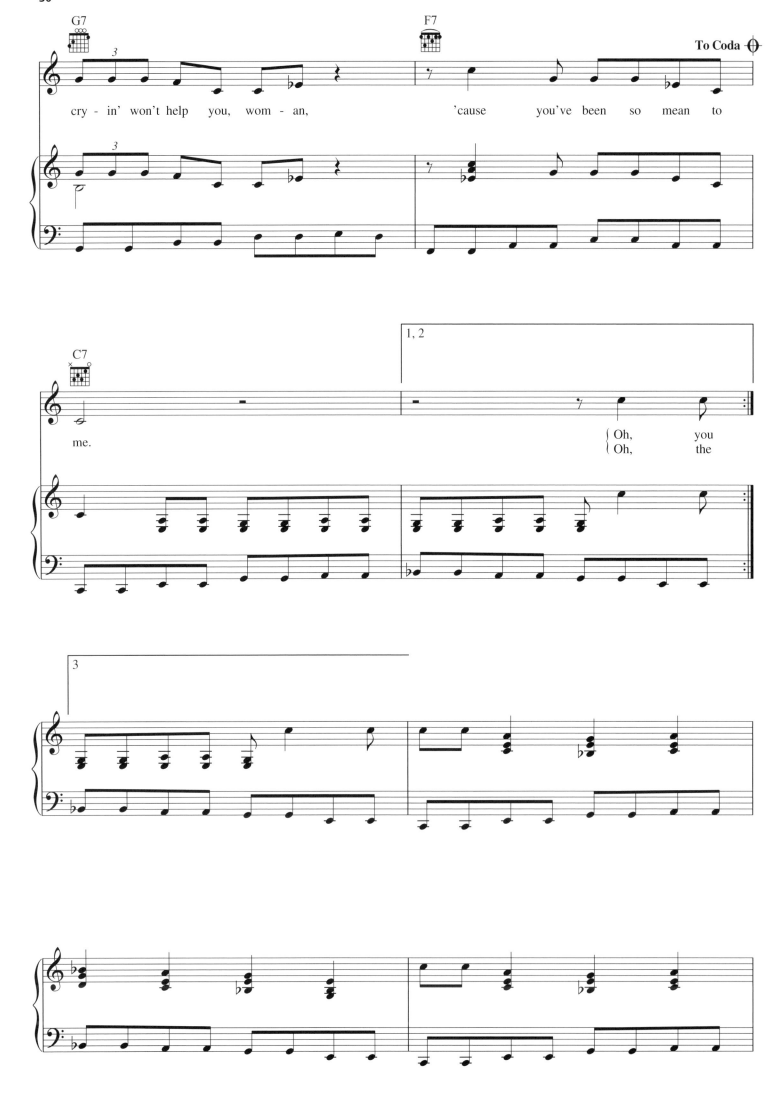

cry - in' won't help you, wom - an, 'cause you've been so mean to

me.

Oh, you
Oh, the

GAMBLER'S BLUES

Words and Music by B.B. KING
and JOHNNY PATE

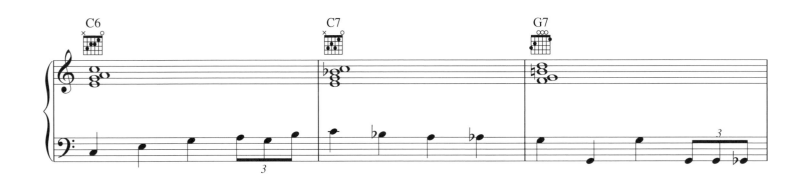

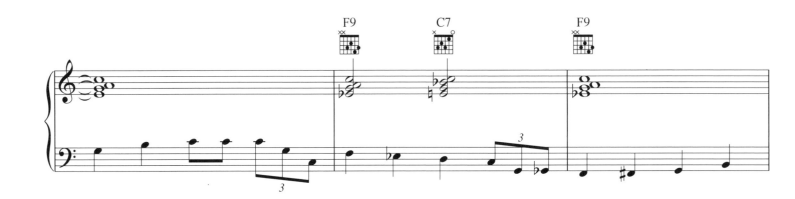

* Recorded a half step higher.

G7   **F9**

love is just a gam - ble, ___ but what-ev - er it is, it's e-nough to drive_ old_

C   **C/E**   **F**   **D7/F♯**   **1, 2 F/G**   **3 F/G**

B. mad. ___ Yes, she

C

left me ear-ly this morn-ing, I don't know the rea-son why. She just got up ear-ly this morn-ing and did-n't e-

C7   **F9**

ven say good-bye. _____ But I love_ you, I love you, you know I love you, ba-

Additional Lyrics

2. They say love is just a proposition, people,
   It's strictly a game of give and take.
   Yeah, they tell me love, love,
   Love is a proposition, people,
   They say it's strictly a game of give and take.
   Whoa, but my woman took all I gave her
   And I'm here to tell to you
   That love proposition stuff's a fake.

3. Oh, I don't claim to be no gambler, people,
   Oh, I don't know much about the dice.
   Yes, I don't claim to be no gambler, people,
   I tell you I don't know much about the dice.
   Oh, but I wait and my baby knows,
   She knows I'm not the kind
   Who's gonna crap out twice.

HELP THE POOR

Words and Music by
CHARLIE SINGLETON

Moderate Latin feel ♩ = 100

Verse:

1. Help the poor;____

2.3. *See additional lyrics*

won't you help poor

me?____

I need help____ from you, ba - by;

ba - by, won't you help poor me.___

I'm in trou - ble; don't you see?___ All___ of your love can save

Repeat ad lib. and fade

me.___ Help the poor;___

Verse 2:
Say you will; say you'll help me on.
I can't make it no further in this world alone.
Baby, I'm beggin', with tears in my eyes,
For your lovin'; don't you realize?
I need help; oh, baby, help poor me.
(To Bridge:)

Verse 3:
Help the poor; baby, help poor me.
Have a heart, won't you, baby; listen to my plea.
I lost my courage till I found you.
You got what it takes, baby, to pull me through.
Help the poor; oh, baby, won't you help poor me.
(To Coda)

HOW BLUE CAN YOU GET

By LEONARD FEATHER

Slow Blues

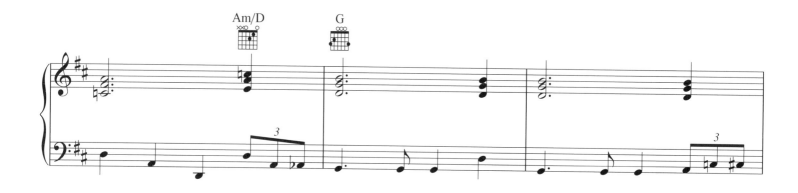

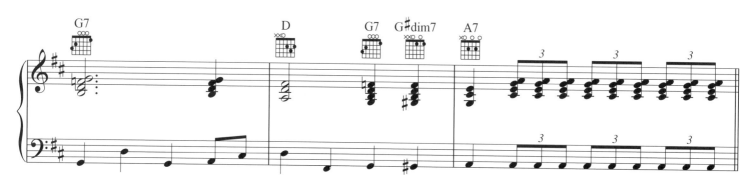

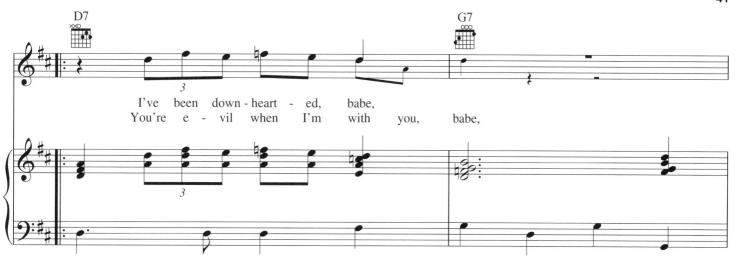

ev - er since the day we met.
and you are jeal - ous when we're a - part.

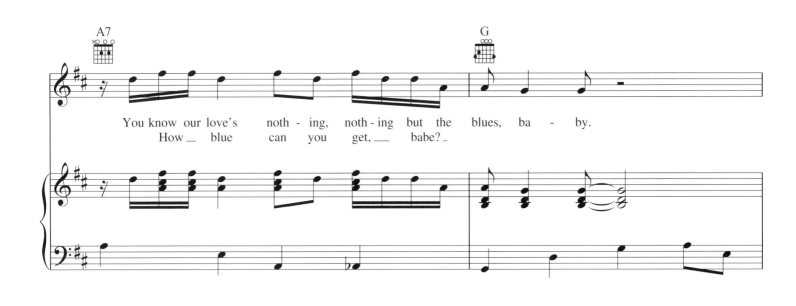

You know our love's noth - ing, noth - ing but the blues, ba - by.
How blue can you get, babe?

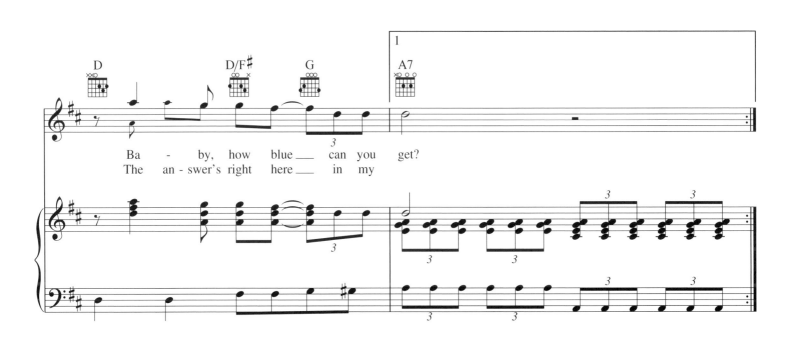

Ba - by, how blue can you get?
The an - swer's right here in my

I NEED YOU SO BAD

Words and Music by B.B. KING
and SAUL BIHARI

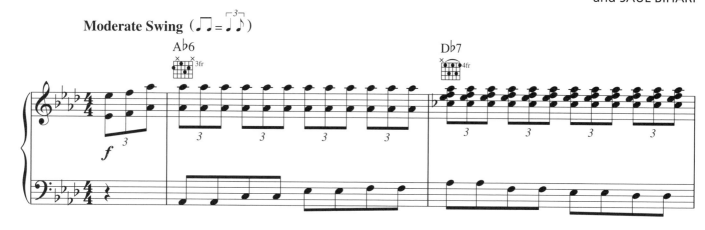

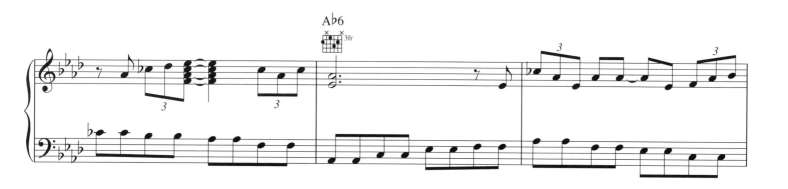

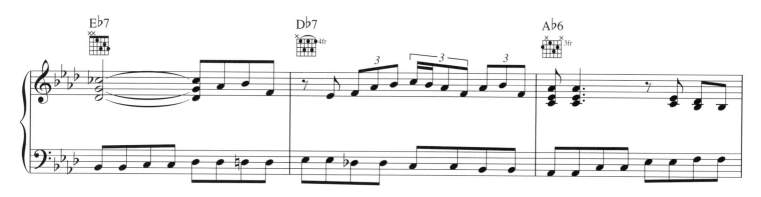

Additional Lyrics

2. Well, I've been looking inside
   Trying to find someone to call my own.
   Yes, I've been looking inside
   Trying to find someone to call my own.
   But without your love, pretty baby,
   I would rather be left alone.

3. I know my luck has been bad,
   It's been bad so many days.
   I know my luck has been bad,
   It's been bad so many days.
   Yes, please come to me, baby,
   Please don't turn my love away.

5. Well, baby, I need you so,
   Yes, baby, honey,
   You know I need you so,
   Well, look right up
   And say you'll take me,
   So I can live just once more.

HUMMINGBIRD

Words and Music by
LEON RUSSELL

NOBODY LOVES ME BUT MY MOTHER

Words and Music by
B.B. KING

Slow Blues

Lead vocal ad lib. "oohs" and "aahs" throughout intro

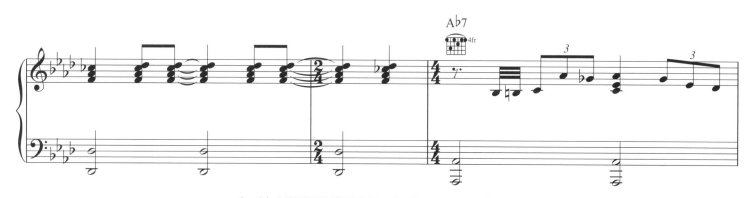

SWEET SIXTEEN

Words and Music by B.B. KING
and JOE BIHARI

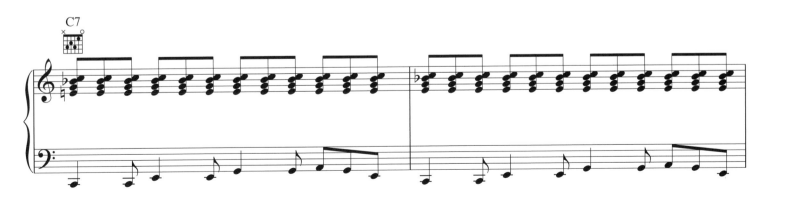

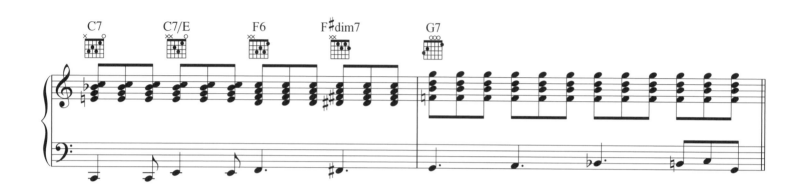

1. When I first met you, ba - by,   ba - by, you were just   sweet six -

2.-6. *(See additional lyrics)*

teen.

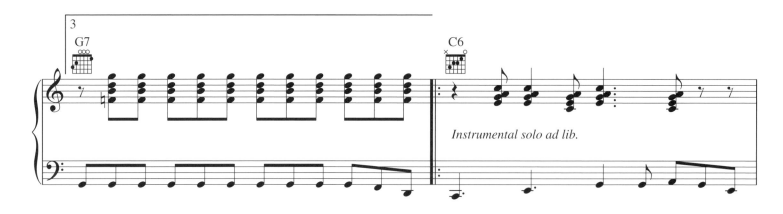

Instrumental solo ad lib.

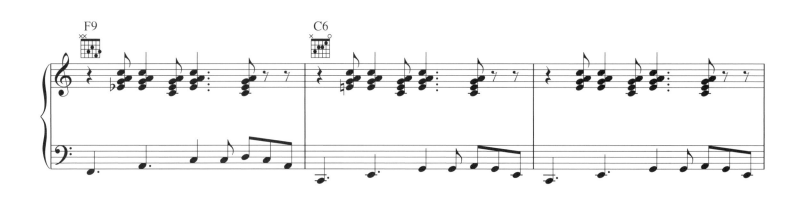

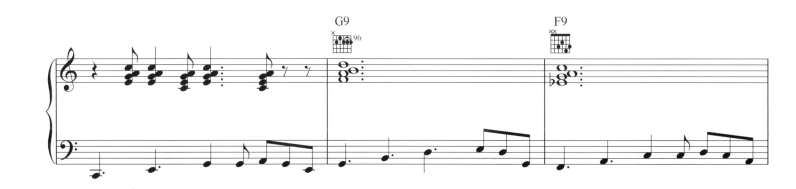

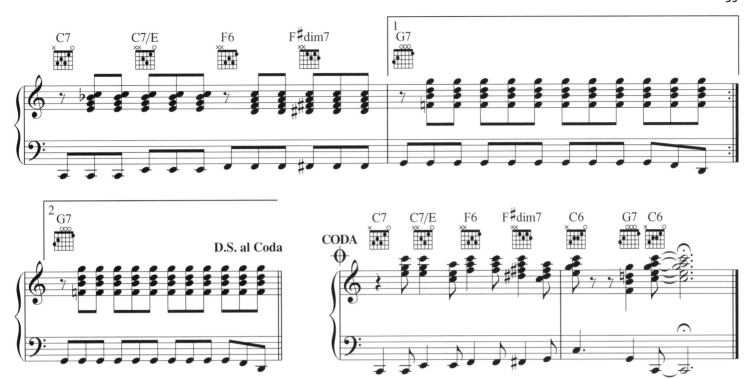

Additional Lyrics

2. But you wouldn't do nothing, baby,
   You wouldn't do anything I asked to.
   You wouldn't do nothing for me, baby,
   You wouldn't do anything I asked to.
   You know you ran away from your home, baby,
   And now you wanna run away from old B., too.

3. You know I love you, babe,
   and I'll do anything you tell me to.
   You know I love you
   and I'll do anything you tell me to.
   Well, there ain't nothing in the world, woman,
   Babe, it ain't nothing,
   Nothing in the world I wouldn't do it for you.

4. I just got back from Vietnam, baby,
   And you know I'm a long, long way from New Orleans.
   I just got back from Vietnam, baby,
   And you know I'm a long, long way from New Orleans.
   I'm having so much trouble, babe,
   I wonder what in the world is gonna happen to me.

5. You can treat me mean, baby,
   But I'll keep on loving you just the same.
   You can treat me mean, baby,
   But I'll keep on loving you just the same.
   But one of these days, baby,
   You're gonna give a lot of money
   To hear someone call my name.

6. Yes, sweet sixteen baby... sweet sixteen...
   Yes, the sweetest thing, baby,
   The sweetest thing I ever seen.
   You know I'm having so much trouble, woman,
   Baby, I wonder,
   Yes, I wonder,
   Baby, I wonder,
   Oh, I wonder what in the world's gonna happen to me.

PAYING THE COST TO BE THE BOSS

Words and Music by
B.B. KING

PLEASE ACCEPT MY LOVE

Words and Music by B.B. KING
and SAUL BIHARI

Moderately

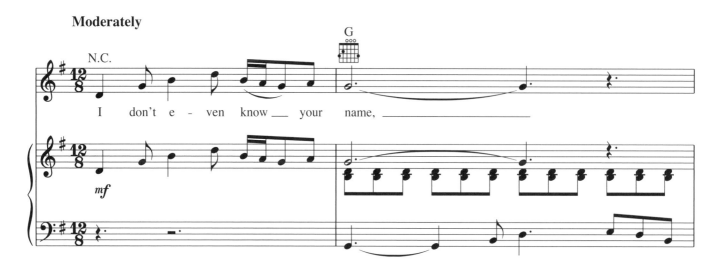

I don't e - ven know ___ your name, _____

but I love you _____ just the same. _____

Dar - ling, __ let me hold _____ your hand _____

RIDING WITH THE KING

Words and Music by
JOHN HIATT

I dreamed I

had a good   job,   I   got well   paid. ___   I blew it all   at the
mis-sion of   mer-cy to the   new fron - tier. ___   He's gon - na check   us all

ROCK ME BABY

Words and Music by B.B. KING
and JOE BIHARI

Rock me, ba - by,
Rock me, ba - by,
Rock me, ba - by,

SWEET LITTLE ANGEL

Words and Music by B.B. KING
and JULES BIHARI

Moderately slow

1. I've got a sweet lit-tle an-gel, __
(2.) ba-by should quit me, __
3. *Guitar solo ad lib.*
4. *(See additional lyrics)*

I love the way she spreads her wings.
I do be-lieve __ I would die.

Yeah, I got a sweet __ lit-tle an-gel, __
Yeah, if my ba-by should quit __ me, __

Additional Lyrics

4. Yes, asked my baby for a nickel, and she gave me a twenty dollar bill.
   Yes, asked my baby for a nickel, and she gave me a twenty dollar bill.
   Yes, you know I asked her to let's go out and have a good time,
   And she bought me a Cadillac Seville.

THREE O'CLOCK BLUES

Words and Music by B.B. KING
and JULES BIHARI

Additional Lyrics

4. Whoa, goodbye everybody, Lord, I believe this is the end.
   Whoa, goodbye everybody, Lord, I believe this is the end.
   Well, you can tell my baby to forgive me for my sins.

THE THRILL IS GONE

Words and Music by ROY HAWKINS
and RICK DARNELL

Moderate Blues

The thrill is gone. ___
The thrill is gone. ___

The thrill has gone ___ a-
It's gone a - way ___ for

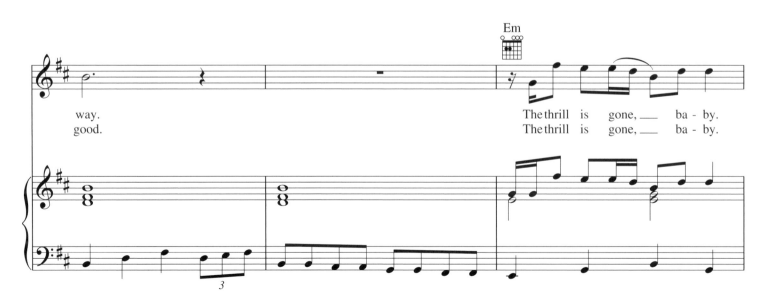

way.
good.

The thrill is gone, ___ ba - by.
The thrill is gone, ___ ba - by.

WHY I SING THE BLUES

Words and Music by B.B. KING
and DAVE CLARK

Well, I've been a - round a long___ time, Umm___ I real - ly paid my

dues.___

1, 2, 3, 4.

5. (Last time)

2. I've

3. I

Extra verses:

4. My kid's gonna grow up, gonna grow up to be a fool
'Cause they ain't got no more room, no more room for him in school,
And everybody wants to know, why I sing the blues.
I say I've been around a long time, yes, I've really paid my dues.

5. Yea, you know the company told me, yes, you're born to lose,
Everybody around feel it, seems like everybody's got the blues.
But I had them a long time, I really, really paid my dues,
You know I ain't ashamed of it, people, I just love to sing the blues.

YOU UPSET ME BABY

Words and Music by B.B. KING
and JULES BIHARI

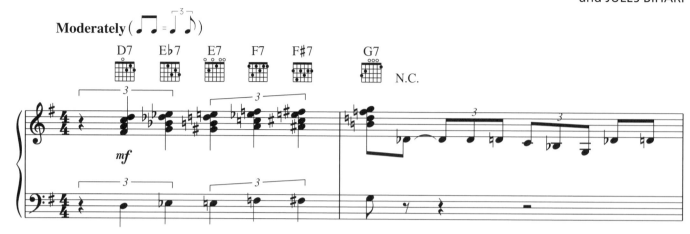

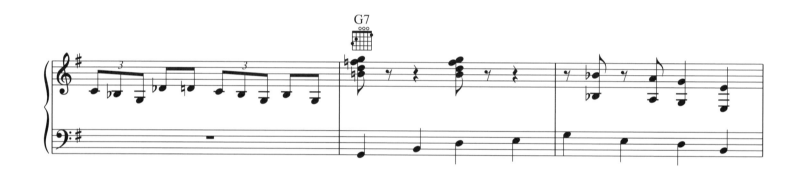

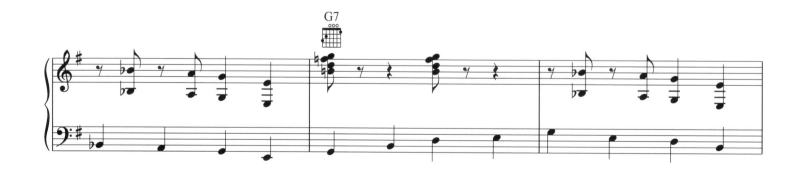

Well,   I've

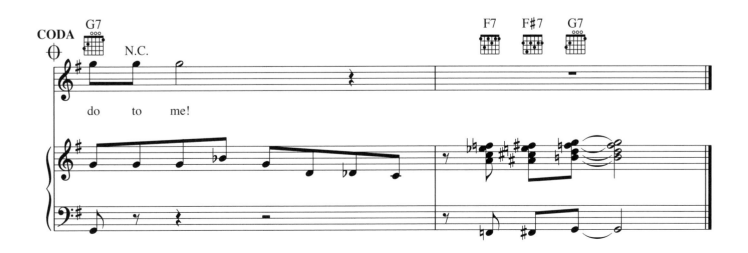

do   to   me!

WOKE UP THIS MORNING

Words and Music by B.B. KING
and JULES BIHARI

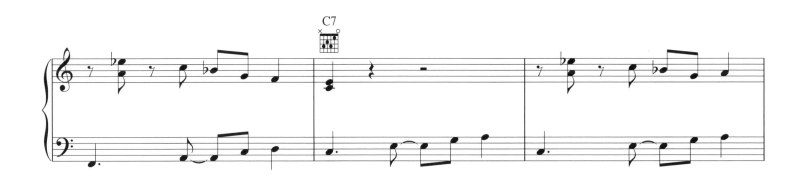

since my ba-by's been gone. Well, __ al - right.
I'm in mis - er